Today's Superst☆

Entertainment

Zac Efron

By Jayne Keedle

Gareth Stevens
Publishing

Please visit our web site at www.garethstevens.com.
For a free color catalog describing our list of high-quality books,
call 1-800-542-2595 (USA) or 1-800-387-3178 (Canada). Our fax: 1-877-542-2596

Library of Congress Cataloging-in-Publication Data
Keedle, Jayne.
  Zac Efron / by Jayne Keedle.
    p. cm. — (Today's superstars : entertainment)
  Includes bibliographical references and index.
  ISBN-13: 978-0-8368-9239-0 (lib. bdg.)
  ISBN-10: 0-8368-9239-9 (lib. bdg.)
    1. Efron, Zac—Juvenile literature. 2. Actors—United States—Biography—
Juvenile literature. I. Title.
PN2287.E395K44   2009
792.02'8092—dc22   2008013763

This edition first published in 2009 by
Gareth Stevens Publishing
A Weekly Reader® Company
1 Reader's Digest Road
Pleasantville, NY 10570-7000 USA

Copyright © 2009 by Gareth Stevens, Inc.

Creative Director: Lisa Donovan
Senior Managing Editor: Lisa M. Herrington
Senior Designer: Keith Plechaty
Senior Editor: Brian Fitzgerald
Photo Researcher: Kim Babbitt

Photo credits: cover, pp. 16, 26 Adam Larkey/Disney Channel; title page, p. 23
New Line/courtesy Everett Collection; p. 5 Scott Brinegar/Disney Channel;
p. 6 Peter Tangen/Disney Channel; p. 7 Jennifer Graylock/AP Images; p. 9
Charlie Gallay/Getty Images; p. 11 Seth Poppel/Yearbook Library; p. 13 Warner
Brothers/courtesy Everett Collection; p. 14 Granada Entertainment/Everett
Collection; pp. 17, 18, 24 Fred Hayes/Disney Channel; p. 20 Tim Mosenfelder/
Getty Images; p. 21 Wire Images/Getty Images; p. 28 Wire Image/Getty Images.

Printed in the United States

1 2 3 4 5 6 7 8 9 10 09 08

Contents

Words in the glossary appear in **bold** type the first time they are used in the text.

Chapter 1

Zac Attack

Mobs of screaming teens clogged the streets of London, England, in August 2007. They were there to meet the cast of *High School Musical*. The young stars were in town to sign DVDs and CDs. The movie's **sequel**, *High School Musical 2*, was already a huge hit in the United States. It was about to **premiere** in England.

Some fans slept out all night for the chance to meet *High School* heartthrob Zac Efron. He plays Troy Bolton, the star of East High's basketball team. Zac was amazed by all the attention. "It's so funny," he told British newspaper the *Daily Mail*. "It's not the 10,000 people screaming. It's when you look down at the one person who is either going crazy or crying."

Great Expectations

Zac's good looks and boy-next-door charm have made him a fan favorite. No one expected *High School Musical* to become a global success. Yet its upbeat message about overcoming peer pressure appealed to teens. They tuned in to watch by the millions. Young fans made the film a hit. Its little-known cast members became stars overnight. "Honestly, I don't think any of us had that high kind of expectations," Zac told PBS Kids. "I think that it was just luck."

Zac is used to being mobbed by fans. A big crowd showed up to see him at the premiere of *High School Musical 2*.

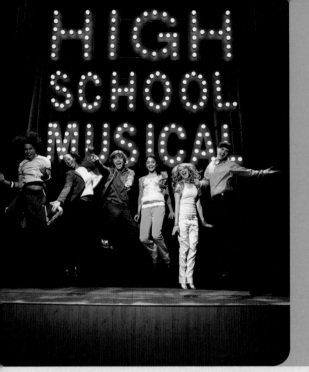

A High Note

High School Musical was an unexpected success. The made-for-TV movie set ratings records when it first aired on the Disney Channel in 2006. It has since attracted a worldwide audience of 200 million and counting. The film cost only about $2 million to make. That's a small budget for a movie. According to one source, Disney has made about $1 *billion* from *High School Musical*. That includes the movies, albums, concert tours, and merchandise!

Teen Idol

Today, even the few people who haven't seen *High School Musical* are likely to recognize Zac. His picture is everywhere, from teen magazines to the cover of *Rolling Stone*. His face appears on lunch boxes, cereal boxes, and wrapping paper. Fans can even see him on tubes of lip balm!

Zac can't make a move without being mobbed by fans. Photographers follow him everywhere. He still can't quite believe that he attracts so much attention. "I had no idea that anyone could ever care," Zac told *Details* magazine. "That happens to, like, big stars."

Fact File

In August 2006, Zac was named Breakout Male Star at the Teen Choice Awards.

Superstar Success

High School Musical made Zac a superstar. It also helped him score other movie roles, beginning with *Hairspray.* Other *High School Musical* stars turned their success into record contracts. Zac focused on his film career instead. For him, making movies is a dream come true.

Zac got his start acting in musicals at a local community theater. He took singing, dancing, and acting lessons to improve his skills. Zac went on hundreds of auditions, hoping for his big break. Until 2006, he considered himself lucky to land even a small part on a TV show. Now everything has changed. Thanks to *High School Musical,* Zac has graduated to the big screen.

In July 2007, Zac showed off the doll of his *Hairspray* character.

Hairspray **director** Adam Shankman says that Zac is "arguably the biggest teen star in America right now." Zac is working hard to turn that fame into a long and successful acting career.

7

Chapter 2

A Star Is Born

Zachary David Alexander Efron was born on October 18, 1987, in San Luis Obispo, California. He grew up in Arroyo Grande, a small town on the coast of California.

Zac is close with his parents and his brother, Dylan, who is four years younger. Growing up, the two boys loved to wrestle. "I think we have the most fun when we're fighting," Zac told *Popstar!* magazine. Their parents, David and Starla, made sure things never got too crazy, though. Both parents worked at a local power plant. One of them was always home when Zac and Dylan returned from school.

Fact File

Zac says the geekiest thing about him is his large comic book collection. In interviews, he's often said he'd like to have superpowers. However, he'd settle for playing the role of a superhero!

Work Before Play

Homework always came before video games. "In my family, if you got a B on your report card, it was 'Shame on you,'" he told *Twist* magazine. "I was always sort of a bookworm. I always tried to get the best grades, and I'm proud of that."

Hooked on Theater

No one in Zac's family had been in show business. However, his parents knew he loved to sing. He learned lyrics fast and had **perfect pitch.** When Zac was 11, his father encouraged him to try out for a local theater production of the musical *Gypsy*.

Zac's parents joined him at the premiere of *High School Musical 2*.

Born to Perform

Zac grew up watching musicals. But he had no formal training in theater, dance, or music. Even so, he managed to land a small part in *Gypsy*. "From day one, I got addicted to being on stage and getting the applause and laughter," he told the *San Luis Obispo Tribune*.

Zac was hooked, all right. He went on to perform in about 40 musicals. He appeared in *The Music Man, Little Shop of Horrors*, and *Peter Pan*, among others. Zac loved playing John in *Peter Pan*. "That was a really fun part because I got to fly around on a 'fly' wire," he explained to *Newsday*. "I was hovering over people in the audience. I actually knocked off a guy's **toupee** once."

Breaking Free

In *High School Musical*, Troy Bolton's teammates give him a hard time about auditioning for the school show. That's something Zac can relate to. His friends didn't understand why he liked theater. "It was kind of like, 'Really? Like, *really*, you have fun acting? Dancing and singing? You really have fun doing that?'" Zac recalled in an interview with *Details* magazine.

Following a Dream

Zac took honors courses in high school and got straight A's. He graduated from Arroyo Grande High School a few months after *High School Musical* came out. "I'm done," he blogged on the *CosmoGIRL!* web site. "!!BOOMSHAKALAKA!! That's the only word I can think of to describe the feeling of never having to do homework again."

Zac was accepted to the University of Southern California. He planned to study filmmaking. But he decided to pursue his acting career instead.

A Helping Hand

Working in community theater gave Zac great acting experience. To improve his performances, he also began taking singing and dance lessons. Zac also joined an **improv** group with his theater friends.

In middle school, Zac took drama classes. His eighth grade drama teacher was impressed with Zac's talent. She put him in touch with her **agent** in Hollywood. That gave Zac the push he needed to give television a try.

Zac was all smiles in his ninth grade yearbook photo.

Chapter 3

No Business Like Show Business

Zac's parents agreed to give him a year to try to break into show business. Every week, his mom drove him to auditions in Los Angeles. The trip was three hours each way. Sometimes, he'd get called back 10 times for a role, only to be rejected.

"For every role that I have done on TV and movies, I've auditioned for 30 or 40," Zac told the *San Luis Obispo Tribune*. "There are several thousand kids out there with brown hair and blue eyes that are my age trying to be in movies. Getting a job is like beating a casino."

Soon, Zac's hard work began to pay off. At first, he got small TV roles. His first part was in an episode of *Firefly* in 2002. In 2003, he actually died in an episode of *ER*!

Zac's luck was not all good, though. He landed parts on three different TV **pilots**. Unfortunately, none of the shows ever made it to television.

Things picked up in 2004. Zac got a guest role on the family drama *Summerland.* The show was about three kids who move in with an aunt after their parents' death. Zac's role as Cameron Bale started out as a one-shot deal. Over time, Cameron became a central character in the show. In season two, Zac became a full-time cast member.

On *Summerland*, Zac (back, second from left) played Cameron Bale. He was the boyfriend of Nikki Westerly, played by Kay Panabaker (far left).

Highs and Lows

Zac's talent as an actor was beginning to draw attention. In 2004, he earned praise for playing a boy with **autism** in the TV movie *Miracle Run*. Zac was nominated for a Young Artist Award for best supporting actor.

Working in show business can be like riding a roller coaster. Zac was riding high when the first big dip came. In 2005, *Summerland* was cancelled. Zac soared again when he landed his first feature-film role in *The Derby Stallion*. He played a 15-year-old who beats the odds and rides an injured racehorse to victory. The film never made it to the big screen, though. Instead, it went straight to DVD.

In *Miracle Run*, Zac played a character who didn't give up on his dreams.

14

Chapter 4

High School Hit

Zac got his biggest break in what everyone thought would be a small film. With *High School Musical,* Disney aimed to make a family comedy about peer pressure. The plot focuses on shy science whiz Gabriella Montez and star jock Troy Bolton. The unlikely couple shocks their friends by trying out for the school musical. The plot twists as their **cliques** try to stop Troy and Gabriella from following their dreams.

Disney decided not to cast big stars in *High School Musical.* Instead, filmmakers held **open auditions.** Zac was one of about 600 teens who tried out. As luck would have it, Zac was paired with Vanessa Hudgens at tryouts. They clicked instantly and won the roles of Troy and Gabriella.

"We're All in This Together"

Other young, talented actors rounded out the *High School Musical* cast. Ashley Tisdale won the role of drama queen Sharpay. Lucas Grabeel was cast as her brother, Ryan. Corbin Bleu earned the part of Chad, Troy's best friend. The role of Gabriella's brainy friend Taylor went to Monique Coleman.

The stars of *High School Musical* (from left): Lucas Grabeel, Monique Coleman, Zac Efron, Ashley Tisdale, Corbin Bleu, and Vanessa Hudgens.

Practice Makes Perfect

The *High School Musical* cast worked together for about six weeks in Salt Lake City, Utah. That included two weeks of rehearsals before they started filming. Zac's days were filled with learning **choreography** and three hours of basketball practice. All that hard work took its toll. "I got twisted ankles, shin splints, and got all beaten up," he told the *Dallas Morning News.*

Kenny Ortega helped Zac learn the dance steps to "Get'cha Head in the Game."

The film's director, Kenny Ortega, was impressed with how hard Zac worked. "He'll sweat for hours in the mirror in prep for a dance number," Ortega told *Details,* "then stay up all night to record a song."

The long hours of practice helped bring the cast together. "We immediately all became fast friends," Zac wrote on Teenmusic.com. "There wasn't a bad seed among any of the kids."

Fact File

Kenny Ortega knows a lot about great dancing. He choreographed the opening ceremony of the 2002 Winter Olympics. He also came up with famous dance scenes in the movies *Dirty Dancing* and *Ferris Bueller's Day Off.*

Hoopla

Zac was definitely acting when he played a basketball star in *High School Musical.* In real life, he wasn't very good at team sports. Zac says that in one season playing on his school's basketball team, he scored only two points.

"I was the worst kid on my sixth grade basketball team," Zac confessed in an online interview for *Newsweek.* "I passed the ball to [the] wrong team and they scored at the buzzer in double overtime to win the championship. It's one of those memories that *still* makes you squirm when you think about it."

In High School Musical, **Troy Bolton (played by Zac) leads the East High Wildcats to the championship.**

The Start of Something New

High School Musical first aired on January 20, 2006. About 7.7 million viewers tuned in. Disney had no idea the movie would attract so many viewers. It soon became clear the network had a major hit on its hands.

Over the next few weeks, *High School Musical* aired five more times. More than 26 million people tuned in watch Troy and the rest of the gang at East High. *High School Musical*'s message of being true to yourself struck a chord with young viewers.

A Taste of Things to Come

It didn't take long for Zac to realize just how much *High School Musical* would change his life. During filming, he and his costars often went to the mall or to movies together. Normally, no one ever bothered them.

Shortly before the film came out, Zac and Ashley Tisdale went to see the Cheetah Girls in concert. The two stars weren't prepared for what awaited them. "The entire audience swarmed Ashley and me," Zac told PBS Kids. Security guards hustled the two teens out the back door for their own safety. It was the first time fans mobbed Zac. It wouldn't be the last.

High School Sing-Along

Of course, there was another big reason for the movie's success. What would a *High School Musical* be without great music? Fans of the movie loved to sing along — and dance — to the film's catchy tunes. "Breaking Free" and "We're All in This Together" were two of the many hits.

In February 2006, nine songs from the movie were on the **music charts** at the same time. That had never happened before in music history. The *High School Musical* sound track became the top-selling album of the year.

Drew Seeley played Troy on the *High School Musical* concert tour.

Credit Where It's Due

Zac has a good singing voice, but he didn't use it much in *High School Musical*. Rehearsals for the dance and basketball scenes kept him out of the recording studio. Canadian actor and singer Drew Seeley filled in for him.

"I sing, like, the beginnings and ends of all the songs," Zac told Digital Spy. Zac never felt comfortable with getting credit for someone else's singing. He has sung all his own songs ever since.

High School Musical was also a hit with **critics**. In August 2007, the film won two Emmys, the top awards for TV shows. The sound track won a Grammy, the highest honor in music.

To build on the film's success, Disney launched a sold-out concert tour. Fans across the country got to see the *High School Musical* stars in person—except for Zac. He had even bigger plans.

Zac and Vanessa Hudgens proudly displayed their Emmy Awards.

Chapter 5

Life Beyond High School

Starring in *High School Musical* gave Zac's career a huge boost. While the rest of the cast was on the concert tour, Zac was in Toronto, Canada. He was working on his next film, *Hairspray.* Zac was cast as Link Larkin, a heartthrob on a 1960s dance show. It was his first role in a major feature film.

Hairspray is a remake of a Broadway show, which was based on the 1988 film. Zac saw both to prepare for his role. The movie tackles some serious subjects, such as **segregation.** But *Hairspray* is also goofy and a lot of fun. Zac saw it as the perfect film for him. "It still has all the fun and excitement that *High School Musical* has," he explained to *USA Today.* "But it also has some deep messages."

Ladies' Choice

Released in July 2007, *Hairspray* was one of the surprise hits of the summer. The feel-good musical made more than $100 million. Zac got good reviews for his singing and acting. He proved he was more than just another teen idol. Zac earned a Young Hollywood Award as "One to Watch" for his performance.

Fact File

Zac wasn't the only breakout young star in *Hairspray*. Costar Nikki Blonsky also made her big screen debut in the film. Like Zac, she earned a "One to Watch" award.

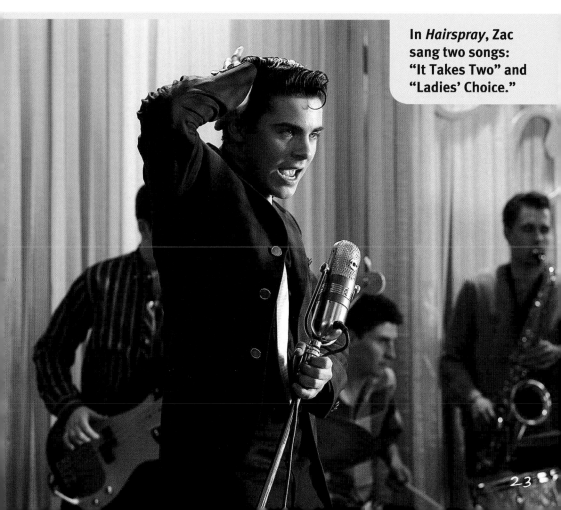

In *Hairspray*, Zac sang two songs: "It Takes Two" and "Ladies' Choice."

On Vacation

After *Hairspray*, Zac went back to the role that made him famous. In *High School Musical 2*, Troy and his friends spend the summer working at a country club.

Amazingly, the second film was a bigger ratings hit than the first. A whopping 17.2 million U.S. viewers saw *High School Musical 2*. At the time it was the most-watched cable television show of all time.

Troy Bolton (played by Zac) and friends celebrated the end of the school year in *High School Musical 2*.

New Directions

Zac has a habit of impressing directors with his talent and hard work. In fact, *Hairspray* director Adam Shankman created the film *Seventeen Again* especially for Zac.

The movie is about a 36-year-old man who wakes up to find he's 17. Zac has played the role of a high school senior before. This time, however, he had to act like a 36-year-old trapped in a 17-year-old's body. How did he prepare? "I tried to do a few things that I learned from my dad," he told MTV. "Things that he thinks are cool but are really dorky."

Happy Endings

In late 2008, Zac went back to *High School* for the last time. Shooting the final film in the series was a happy reunion. "It's, like, not even work," Zac said. "We just have the time of our lives out there."

Unlike the previous films, *High School Musical 3* will be shown in theaters. Zac told MTV, "It's going to be a good way to go out with a bang."

Fact File

Hannah Montana star Miley Cyrus appears near the end of *High School Musical 2*. She can be seen dancing by the pool during the final song, "All for One." She is onscreen for only two seconds!

Zanessa?

In 2006, Zac and Vanessa Hudgens won the Teen Choice Award for Best Chemistry. The prize was awarded for the way their characters got along in *High School Musical*. It didn't take long for the actors to feel a magical connection in real life, too.

The press often linked Zac with Vanessa. Some magazines started calling them "Zanessa." For a long time, the costars said they were just good friends. In May 2007, a photographer snapped pictures of the pair in Hawaii. There was no denying the romance. Still, Zac dodged questions about their relationship. He prefers to keep his private life to himself.

Vanessa and Zac are a popular couple, both onscreen and off.

Dancing to Different Tunes

Zac signed on to make two other films in 2008. *High School Musical* director Kenny Ortega will direct Zac in a remake of the 1984 film *Footloose*. It's the story of a teen who moves to a small town where dancing is banned. Despite the plot, the film is a musical with lots of dancing.

Zac's other movie project, *Me and Orson Welles*, gave him a break from musicals. "I love doing musicals, don't get me wrong," he explained to *USA Today*. "But I'm an actor at heart. I'd like to try more adventurous roles."

Fact File

Zac is a health nut. To stay in shape, he works out at the gym every day. At home in Arroyo Grande, he takes early morning runs with his two Australian shepherds, Dreamer and Puppy.

Coping With Fame

Tabloids are full of stories about teen stars gone wild. Zac has given them little to write about. He lives alone in a two-bedroom apartment in Los Angeles. He doesn't go to nightclubs. He doesn't drink, smoke, or do drugs—and he doesn't hang out with people who do.

Zac knows he can count on his family and lifelong friends to keep him grounded. "I come home, and it's a reality check," Zac said in an interview with 7M Pictures.

In *Me and Orson Welles,* Zac's character has a chance meeting with famed director Orson Welles. The event changes the character's life. Will the film set Zac on a new path, too? "In a few years, when I do more adult projects, my fans will also be a little more mature," he told *Newsweek.* "So it'll be fun to grow up with the fans."

For now, Zac isn't concerned about the future. "It's really easy to worry about being pigeonholed in teen stardom," he told *USA Today.* "I'm having fun right now. And I hope I can continue to work, because it's a blessing and I love it."

Zac met Kevin Bacon at an award show in January 2008. Bacon was the star of the original *Footloose.*

Time Line

1987 — Zachary David Alexander Efron is born on October 18, in San Luis Obispo, California.

1998 — Appears in his first play, a local theater production of the musical *Gypsy*.

2002 — Makes his first TV appearance, on the science fiction series *Firefly*.

2004 — Lands a regular role as Cameron Bale on the WB series *Summerland*; stars in the TV movie *Miracle Run*.

2006 — Stars as Troy Bolton in *High School Musical*; graduates from Arroyo Grande High School; wins three Teen Choice Awards and an Emmy Award for *High School Musical*.

2007 — Stars as Link Larkin in the feature film *Hairspray*; returns as Troy Bolton in *High School Musical 2*; wins two more Teen Choice Awards; signs on to star in *Footloose*.

2008 — Appears in *Seventeen Again* and *High School Musical 3*; films *Me and Orson Welles*.

Glossary

agent—a person who represents an actor or singer and helps him or her find work

autism—a disorder that affects the brain, especially communication and social skills

choreography—dance routines

cliques—small groups of friends who exclude others

critics—in entertainment, people whose job is to give their opinions about movies, TV shows, or music

director—a person who is in charge during the filming of a movie or TV show

improv—the art of performing without any practice

music charts—lists of the most popular songs or albums

open auditions—tryouts for roles in movies, plays, or TV shows that anyone can attend

perfect pitch—the ability to recognize and sing a given musical note well

pilots—test episodes of possible new television shows

premiere—to be shown in public for the first time

segregation—keeping people separate because of race

sequel—a film that continues the story of an earlier film

tabloids—newspapers that focus on stories about celebrities

toupee—a wig that covers a bald spot

To Find Out More

Books

Hairspray: The Novel. Tracey West (Price Stern Sloan, 2007)

High School Musical: The Junior Novel. N.B. Grace (Disney Press, 2006)

High School Musical 2: The Junior Novel. N.B. Grace (Disney Press, 2007)

DVDs

The Derby Stallion (Echo Bridge Home Entertainment, 2007)

Hairspray (New Line Home Video, 2007)

High School Musical (Walt Disney Video, 2006)

High School Musical 2 (Walt Disney Video, 2007)

Web Site

tv.disney.go.com/disneychannel/originalmovies/highschoolmusical
Check out the official web site for *High School Musical* and *High School Musical 2.*

Index

About the Author

Jayne Keedle is a freelance writer and editor. Born in England, she lives along the Niantic River in Connecticut with her husband, Jim; stepdaughter, Alma; a chocolate Lab named Snuffles; and Phoenix the cat.